# WHISPERS ON MY SKIN

Charlene Smith ©

January, 2012, updated September, 2016

Cambridge, Massachusetts

www.charlenesmithwriter.com

Award winning journalist and author, Charlene Smith achieved international renown after she campaigned for better rights for rape survivors after she was raped and stabbed in her home by a stalker. This trauma came after years of covering conflict in troubled countries and of creating programs to help journalists cope with Post Traumatic Stress Syndrome.

Her campaign to ensure anti-retroviral medication for rape survivors saw her initiate and then work with the Centers of Disease Control on their protocol for post-exposure prophylaxis after sexual assault. This protocol, now used in most countries of the world is to improve treatment and care of rape survivors and in particular to prevent HIV. It was released in 2004.

Charlene has reported on conflict on three continents and first led her to research trauma and to train for and become a certified trauma counselor.

She has been invited by governments, conferences, universities, medical schools, and organizations around the world to give her views on trauma, sexual violence, HIV and AIDS.

It was her insistence on the term 'survivor' instead of 'victim' that saw a global change in rape terminology.

A certified trauma counselor with extensive experience in counseling journalists who report in war zones and other survivors of trauma, whether rape survivors, families of murder victims, those battling terminal illnesses she has received international awards for this work. She has counseled thousands of rape survivors, and their families, journalists, military veterans, those incarcerated, and others that have experienced violent harm. She is acknowledged as a global expert.

In her voluntary work over decades in prisons on two continents has revealed the very high percentage of those jailed for violent crimes were raped years before they committed the crimes for which they are now in jail for many years or life. They were most often raped as young boys by fathers, grandfathers, aunts, priests or teachers – always someone they should have been able to trust. And never received help. This inner rage finally turned outward with devastating consequences for them and others. It is significant too that rapists conceal their crime once incarcerated, especially if they harmed a child – these are the prisoners most likely to be killed by their fellow inmates.

Decades later these big men cry like the small child they once were when they were harmed and there was no one to listen. Perhaps if someone had, later harm could have been prevented.

The most common issue those who have experienced violence is around intimacy, Touch, once so beloved, once the carrier of soothing intimacy, now feels dangerous.

*The enemy without, becomes the enemy within.*

One of the most common challenges Charlene experiences from trauma survivors is how to have a loving sexual relationship after experiencing violent harm. "It's amazingly easy to heal and move forward once you change your mind set, but it is a choice you need to make. You can allow yourself to be pathologized and become a primary contributor to the lucrative pharmaceuticals industry – in other words if you feel soothed being given a diagnosis and a fist fill of pills, then that's fine, but healing will be years slower, if ever.

"You can choose to be self-pitying and angry, always demanding of attention and sympathy, or you can begin living the life you deserve – this all sounds like tough talking, but it's not, it is born of decades of experience.

"Do not allowed those that harm to own or crush you. The ways to do this are many, some seem so obvious you may feel like dismissing them – don't. It takes bricks and mortar, timber and steel, glass and roofing, small nails and screws, bits of glue and fiber, to create a home, don't go for the large and neglect the small, because it is the small that most often holds the st

This little book tells how she and others, male and female, have coped. It quotes from research and deals with issues around domestic violence, gang rape, pregnancy after rape, conflict, war, pornography, eating disorders, some religious views, post- traumatic stress syndrome, helping those who love you, and most importantly, it gives practical steps to restore intimacy.

It draws from the experience of others, some will be like your experience, or you may find yourself saddened by others, but these are their stories and your negative response to any makes someone feel as unworthy and damaged as you once felt – compassion is a good exercise, those that harm lack it, it is important that we who were once harmed practice it.

Persistently look and listen for words of inspiration, they often come from unexpected people and places, and usually when you most need them.

*If you live your life fully, you will die only once. But if you are scared of every step, fear will kill you day after day, Paulo Coelho*

*the light that came to lucille clifton*

*came in a shift of knowing*

*when even her fondest sureties*

*faded away. it was the summer*

*she understood that she had not understood*

*and was not mistress even*

*of her own off eye, then*

*the man escaped throwing away his tie and*

*the children grew legs and started walking and*

*she could see the peril of an*

*unexamined life.*

*she closed her eyes, afraid to look for her*

*authenticity*

*but the light insists on itself in the world;*

*a voice from the nondead past started talking,*

*she closed her ears and it spelled out in her hand*

*"you might as well answer the door, my child,*

*the truth is furiously knocking." – Lucille Clifton, Selected Poems*

# Table of Contents

# THE DEEPEST WOUND

*The deepest wound violent criminals inflict is not the path of a knife or the imprint of a hand, it is a psychological assault, and courts rarely take that into account.*

Loving sexual relationships are important for us to function effectively. Problems after rape in accepting loving intimate touch are a component of Post-Traumatic Stress Syndrome and so we have to make a decision, we can allow the rapist or rapists to control our lives and forego loving, intimate relationships or we need to defy those that harmed us and relearn that touch is healing and good for us.

Take back your life. Realize that fears around sex mean that you are keeping the rapist or rapists in our life, while pushing away those who love you. Do not help the rapist to harm you long after the rapist has left and forgotten you. Work on getting rid of the rapist. And in truth it is not as hard as you now believe if you read this book carefully and follow the steps given. And of course, go to a physician and check that there are no physical obstacles to you experiencing intimacy again with your partner; for some even that physical exam may be challenging so read through this first.

Start implementing the suggestions and then go to the doctor knowing that to him or her there is nothing sexual about your body – he or she sees your body as a painter sees a canvas, intriguing for the possibilities it may reveal, but definitely not a source of desire. They want you to heal. This is their job, help them to help you.

Some people say, it is so unfair that I have to do all this work after being raped.

Is it unfair?

It's unfair because we wonder why we should do so much hard work after being harmed.

Yet it is not unfair because this is our only life and only we can make it better. We can't ask others to do this; it is our life, our work to make this a life worth living.

Reading this book is your big chance to change your life. Don't make excuses to delay it. Don't blame anyone else. Accept responsibility. Start doing everything you need to now, the list I give later in this book looks exhausting, but actually it will be more fun than you can begin to imagine, as you do one step, then the next you will find you gain in energy and enthusiasm. One woman reported after just a few steps that everyone around her started saying, "it's not possible that someone can change so much in just two weeks," but she did.

Another woman carried such shame she wouldn't even post her picture on Facebook, I suggested that perhaps part of her new act of self-love was to smile out at the world. And so she put her photograph up on Facebook. I laughed when I read the astonished views of those who had known her long. She said a friend phoned to ask if her page had been hacked, she could not believe that this timid rape survivor was now lifting her head and smiling at the world.

Let's look at where you are now and try to understand why you are experiencing so many troubling emotions.

Death comes in many forms. It can be a slow emotional disassembling when women after a rape are treated as subhuman by hospitals, doctors and nurses. I have asked medical staff to touch rape survivors when first they encounter them, even if the rapist has urinated them on or they are bloodied. What we often experience after acts of violence against us is an emotional death. We feel as though we have crossed to the other side, that there is no way back. We see others laughing, holding hands, embracing, we cannot imagine how we could ever do that again.

I ask trauma specialists and medical staff to touch us: 'If she is covered in blood or mud then put on plastic aprons and rubber gloves, but touch her. The perpetrator tried to remove our humanity, we need you to help give it back to us.' Indeed, I believe that if we are not touched, often, in the first twelve hours after a violent attack and made to talk in detail of the event while we are still numb, within three days we will begin clamming up and rejecting touch. Fear first attacks our throats, and then implants itself in our emotions, drying them even as they become more visible than at any other time in our lives.

*Never demean your pain.* This trauma is the worst thing that happened to you. Acknowledge your pain, assert your right to grieve, and do it. Then say: now I need to move on and build a better life. How do I do that? The truth is none of us knows. We just need to begin walking, step by step, towards the light until, as we get closer, we realize that the light was always within us. We are the light. We hold our destiny.

I don't believe anyone is ordinary. To me, the word *extraordinary* is an acknowledgement that each of us contains within us the seeds of wisdom and the ability to perform remarkable deeds.

Sometimes pain unlocks that potential.

What can we learn from pain?

We can hang our heads in self-pity and twist our hearts into bitterness. Or we can advance toward the fear that threatens to conquer us, so in this book we learn that:

**Rape is not sex.** *Sex is not rape.*

The person who raped me would have had more sexual gratification from putting his penis into a plughole. In some rapes women are told at gunpoint to 'move up and down'. In what definition is that sex? The fact that most rapists battle with erections show that it is not even giving them pleasure.

A gang member who raped the relative of a famous political leader said to the deeply traumatized woman, 'I am a great admirer of your relative.' Raping her was an achievement for him because he could never - in his eyes - aspire to socialize with anyone linked to such a high-ranking official, so rape became a way of attaining status.

In the United States, the Bureau of Justice classifications are:

**Rape** - Forced sexual intercourse including both psychological coercion as well as physical force. Forced sexual intercourse means penetration by the offender(s). Includes attempted rapes, male as well as female victims, and both heterosexual and same sex rape. Attempted rape includes verbal threats of rape.

**Sexual assault** - A wide range of victimizations, separate from rape or attempted rape. These crimes include attacks or attempted attacks generally involving unwanted sexual contact between victim and offender. Sexual assaults may or may not involve force and include such things as grabbing or fondling. It also includes verbal threats.

The definition of rape by the BoJ is backward compared to that found in other countries, in Britain, as an example, the rapist needs touch only the tip of the labia. To regard only actual penetration is to disregard the amount of erectile dysfunction in rapists and that some rape is perpetrated by women. In most international terminology too, sexual assault is considered rape.

The Centers for Disease Control in Atlanta, Georgia has far better definitions, it is worth publishing an abridged version because you may be uncertain, given the BoJ's pitiful explanation of whether what happened to you can be labelled rape:

*Sexual violence is a sexual act committed without a person's freely given consent [and] is divided into the following types:*
- *Completed or attempted forced penetration of a victim*
- *Completed or attempted alcohol/drug-facilitated penetration of a victim*
- *Completed or attempted forced acts in which a victim is made to penetrate ... someone*
- *Completed or attempted alcohol/drug-facilitated acts in which a victim is made to penetrate... someone*
- *Non-physically forced penetration after a person is pressured verbally or through intimidation or misuse of authority to consent or acquiesce*
- *Unwanted sexual contact*
- *Non-contact unwanted sexual experiences*
      *Completed or attempted forced penetration of a victim — includes completed or attempted unwanted vaginal (for women), oral, or anal insertion through use of physical force or threats to bring physical harm toward or against the victim. Examples include*
- *Pinning the victim's arms*
- *Using one's body weight to prevent movement or escape*
- *Use of a weapon or threats of weapon use*
- *Assaulting the victim*
      [this may happen if the victim] *was too intoxicated (e.g., incapacitation, lack of consciousness, or lack of awareness) through voluntary or involuntary use of alcohol or drugs. Completed or attempted forced acts in which a victim is made to penetrate a perpetrator or someone else — includes situations when the victim was made, or there was an attempt to make the victim, sexually penetrate a perpetrator or someone else without the victim's consent because the victim was physically forced or threatened with physical harm... Completed or attempted alcohol or drug-facilitated acts... Nonphysically forced penetration which occurs after a person is pressured verbally, or through intimidation or misuse of authority, to consent or submit to being penetrated - examples include being worn down by someone who repeatedly asked for sex or showed*

*they were unhappy; feeling pressured by being lied to, or being told promises that were untrue; having someone threaten to end a relationship or spread rumors; and sexual pressure by use of influence or authority.*

*Unwanted sexual contact – intentional touching, either directly or through the clothing, of the genitalia, anus, groin, breast, inner thigh, or buttocks of any person without his or her consent, or of a person who is unable to consent or refuse.*

*Unwanted sexual contact can be perpetrated against a person or by making a person touch the perpetrator.*

*Unwanted sexual contact could be referred to as "sexual harassment" ..., such as a school or workplace.*

*Noncontact unwanted sexual experiences - does not include physical contact of a sexual nature between the perpetrator and the victim. This occurs against a person without his or her consent, or against a person who is unable to consent or refuse. Some acts of non-contact unwanted sexual experiences occur without the victim's knowledge. This type of sexual violence can occur in many different settings, such as school, the workplace, in public, or through technology. Examples include unwanted exposure to pornography or verbal sexual harassment (e.g., making sexual comments)."*

Men – and those women - who are sexually aggressive are often good looking. They appear successful, and may be in marriages or relationships, but inside they feel inadequate. In South Africa a Community Information and Education Transparency (CIET) report in June 2000 showed that of more than 6,000 people surveyed, two percent more educated and employed men raped than those less advantaged.

In the United States a woman increases her risk of sexual assault three-fold by attending college. We have to only look at well-publicized cases of sexual assault at

Stanford and exclusive public schools, allegations against comedian Bill Cosby or Fox network head, Roger Ailes, as examples, of instances of sexual violence by prominent men who use their status to lure women or boys and then stave off complaints or lawsuits often by saying to those they abuse, "no one will believe you because I am (celebrity or famous person name, a priest, a CEO, etc.)

Because these men feel worthless (even though they may outwardly appear successful), they often experience erectile problems, which is why laws across the world that describe rape as using the penis as a weapon are so wrong. Very often those 'weapons' are limp; erections are difficult to attain, and more difficult to retain - and so women, men or children sexually assaulted, get beaten or have objects forced into them as punishment for the rapist's inadequacies.

After experiencing violence, we may feel as though we have entered a secret room that we knew was always there but to which entry was denied. Within that dark and fearful room are dozens of men, women and children; many are people you admire. They sit in silence, believing they are alone despite the claustrophobia of their overwhelming presence. People, who experience other violent trauma, experience some of this post-crime or post-war loneliness, but no crime carries greater stigma, shame and silence than sexual violence. It is hard to speak out but absolutely necessary for our emotional health.

Rape pathologist Dr. Karien Muller, when she gives

talks, says to her audience: 'I now want you to turn to the person sitting to the left of you and give them a detailed description of your most recent sexual experience.' There is usually a stunned silence from the audience, and then nervous giggles.

And then she says, 'Right, now you have a small sense of how a rape survivor feels when she has to sit before a stranger and describe not a loving sexual encounter, but a barbarous act where many perversions may have been performed.'

After I was raped and stabbed I wrote to a friend:

"I think one of the things that most do not see is that although I have been strong, and am fighting to get the drugs for other women and children and to bring down the statistics, inside I am wounded.

"I told my mother that if I close my eyes and visualize my body it is a body without form, no hair or sexual features, my head is down, my arms behind me, as when he bound me, and across my body are lacerations as if I have been whipped, they crisscross my body, they have torn the skin, but I am not bleeding. I hope this does not sound too strange to you. In one way the fact that those wounds are not bleeding tells me I know they will heal. The lack of form, I suppose, tells me that he tried to remove my sexuality and indeed, for now, it is gone." It took deliberate work to get it back, and in the process I rediscovered myself anew, and developed deeper respect for the power of a good relationship.

Open the curtains of that room, let in the light, help others to break down the doors and destroy the rapist's power.

# EXERCISE

Try this introspective exercise. Do it in a quiet space and take your time. After you've finished, put it away. After reading this book, or in three months, do it again and compare the two – has anything changed? Has something improved? Something worsened? How you can improve the answers.

1. Age
2. Birthplace
3. Where I live now
4. Place I was happiest and year/s – one sentence on why
5. Place I was unhappiest and why
6. The person I love most – and why
7. The things that drive me crazy – name 3
8. My best feature
9. I am most grateful for …. (complete)
10. If I could change …. (complete)
11. The goal I would most like to achieve in the year ahead
12. The goal I would most like to achieve in the next 3 months
13. What makes the person I love most, happy?
14. How would you describe courage? Please name one person you consider courageous.
15. The last time I was kind to a stranger was …. I did …. to make them happy. How I felt after.
16. What I would like people to feel after interacting with me.
17. How I think people feel after interacting with me.

# You're not alone: some statistics

Police ineptitude in the investigation of rape – globally – is staggering; it is the one crime, everywhere in the world that is least likely to result in an arrest or conviction. In 2009/10[1], police recorded 43,579 sexual offences in England and Wales, encompassing rape, sexual assault and sexual activity with children. In South Africa the Department of Justice said seven per cent of the 54,000 reported rapes in 1998 were prosecuted, and of those only one percent resulted in convictions.

On average[2], 24 people a minute are victims of rape, physical violence, or stalking by an intimate partner in the United States, according to the Centers for Disease Control and Prevention. Over the course of a year, that equals more than 12 million women and men. Research released in December, 2011 noted that more than 1 million women reported being raped in a year and over 6 million women and men were victims of stalking in a year.

In 1960, according to the Bureau of Justice there were 17,190 cases of "forced rape" (is there any other kind?) in a population of 179-million people. By 2012, and a population slightly less than three times bigger – or 313-million people – reports of rape had shot up eight times to 84,376 – still a relatively low figure for such a large population. However, the Bureau of Justice lumps together rape with robbery and aggravated assault to create a category called 'violent victimization' which effectively masks rape statistics; in 2010 it reported '1.4 million serious violent victimizations.' [3] Why feminists do not challenge this bizarre and outmoded categorization by this federal department is unknown.

The United States Bureau of Justice lumps together rape with robbery and aggravated assault to create a category called 'violent victimization' which effectively masks rape statistics; in 2010 it reported '1.4 million serious violent victimizations.' [4] According to the Rape, Abuse, and Incest National Network (RAINN) every two minutes someone is sexually assaulted in the United States, with around 213,000 people experiencing sexual violence each year.[5] As you can see, the United States is hopeless in tracking sexual assault and yet strangely despite increased reporting and more women talking openly against perpetrators, there has been no concomitant funding toward better research and more reliable statistics – which in turn would lead to more effective policing, court cases, medical and societal support and help.

The National Intimate Partner and Sexual Violence Survey, or NISVS from CDC monitors sexual violence, stalking and intimate partner violence victimization in the United States. (For this section I have retained the CDC's use of the word victim although I disapprove of it, survivor is more appropriate – the word victim is in itself victimizing and discriminatory.)

Key findings in the NISVS 2010 Summary Report include:

WOMEN:

Nearly 1 in 5 women in the USA has been raped at some time in her life.

One in 4 women was a victim of severe physical violence by an intimate partner.

One in 6 women has experienced stalking to the extent that she believed that she or someone close to her would be harmed or killed. Stalking victimization is facilitated by technology, such as unwanted phone calls and text messages. It has become a significant problem on social media.

Almost 70 percent of female victims experienced some form of intimate partner violence before the age of 25.

Approximately 80 percent of female victims of sexual assault were first raped before age 25. Female victims of violence are significantly more likely to report physical and mental health problems than women who never experience harm. Across all forms of violence (sexual violence, stalking, intimate partner violence), most victims knew the perpetrator (often an intimate partner or acquaintance and seldom a stranger).

MEN[6]:

One in 7 men has experienced severe physical violence by an intimate partner at some point in their lifetime.

One in 19 men has experienced stalking at some point in which they felt very fearful or believed that they or someone close to them would be harmed or killed.

Almost 53 percent of male victims' experience intimate partner violence for the first time before age of 25

More than a quarter of male rape victims were first raped when they were 10-years-old or younger.

Male victims of violence are significantly more likely to report physical and mental health problems than those who have never been harmed.

The report underscores violence as a major public health burden and demonstrates how violence can have impacts that last a lifetime. For instance, women who have experienced harm are more likely to have long-term health problems, including irritable bowel syndrome, diabetes, frequent headaches, chronic pain, and difficulty sleeping. Nearly twice as many women who were victims of violence reported having asthma, compared to women who did not report violence victimization. I, as an example, started experiencing serious asthma for the first time after I was raped.

Weight issues are also significant with those raped, either a tendency to obesity or disorders including bulimia, anorexia, etc.

# Your Relationship

Great relationships are characterized by sympathetic joy, which is a translation of the Pali and Sanskrit word Muditā "the pleasure that comes from delighting in other people's well-being."

Does your partner, friends, fellow students or work colleagues help you feel good about you? Distance yourself from those who diminish you with faint praise or no praise, who criticize you, who gossip about others (because you can bet they gossip about you), who have nothing nice to say about others, who measure success in materialistic terms eg. the size of your house, the clothes you wear, your weight, etc.

Surround yourself with those who find the good in life and in others, because they will see what is most positive in you and show pleasure in their relationship with you. These are the people you most enjoy spending time with and when you leave a meeting with them you feel good about life.

Martin Seligman in his book *Flourish*, says there are four possible responses when someone shares something with you about their success: active constructive, passive constructive, passive destructive, and active destructive. If something good happens to you and you share it with someone, a passive constructive response is, "That's nice." Occasionally there is a passive destructive response such as being ignored when you share your good news. Active destructive is critical, for example, "You didn't earn that promotion."

What enriches a relationship is an active constructive response, when the person who hears of our success is sincerely happy for us. An active constructive response shows generosity of spirit and eagerness to hear more details about their good news. Celebrating the triumphs in life, from the small seemingly trivial ones to those that are more significant, strengthens the bond. Being genuinely enthusiastic in our response to our partner's good fortune has a weighty impact on them. Here's a good example of an active constructive response.

Mark: "I've been selected to receive an award because of my leadership and high performance."

Megan: "That's great! You've worked so hard for this. We must bust out a bottle of champagne to celebrate. I am so proud of you I could pop. Tell me all about it"

Megan is sincere about her enthusiasm about Mark's success, rather than envious and competitive. She is happy to have him speak of the details leading up to the good news, how he worked towards promoting the conditions that gave rise to the success and what it means to him. For Mark to have Megan rejoice in his good fortune with him builds their trusting bond.

Something even deeper happens, when we show sincere pleasure in another's success, we feel joy too. When we act to give pleasure to another, it enhances our dopamine and endorphin activity. Even the simple act of standing before flowers and thinking, "would she prefer roses or lilies?" activates our pleasure centers because we are not only reflecting on what would make our friend happy, but too, what gives pleasure to us.

Great relationships occur when we give our time, attention, and care to another. We love our children so much not because of the cute things they say or do, but those long nights when they are ill and we hold their fevered little bodies close to ours willing the sickness to rather enter us.

Happiness is created through selflessness matched with self-love.

Too much caregiving can exhaust and drain you. Happiness occurs when we discover the middle ground between giving, receiving, and actively working to replenish ourselves.

A benefit of romantic partnerships is support when difficult life circumstances befall us. Our partner can be there in our time of need when dark events happen, to be sympathetic and provide a shoulder to cry on. Sincere support softens the blow and helps us to get through it.

We want our partner or friend to be proud of our achievements, and to celebrate with us to magnify the joy.

A male friend said, "I want to be admired." He is not unique, we all want that even if it is just one aspect of our personality: "Wow, Jill, you make the best tacos ever."

Envy can be cultivated or starved. When we are aware of the negative effect that envy has on our relationship, we can use that awareness to be inspired to become a bigger person, rather than diminish anyone. "You know, Jill, your tacos would be a whole lot better if you used less cilantro. And you might also consider using fish instead of beef."

Shelly Gable, professor of psychology at University of California, Santa Barbara, in her article, *Will You Be There for Me When Things Go Right?* (The Journal of Personality and Social Psychology 2006) says that how we celebrate is more predictive of strong relationships than how we fight. She writes about the frequent positive exchanges that characterize good romantic partnerships. The loving notes, the thanks you say, the use of 'please' when you ask, the regret you express, the admissions that you were wrong. The surprise gifts. Dates that you dress up for. And the occasional text that says, "I was watching a couple argue today, and I am so grateful we don't do that. I want to thank you for your great temperament and for the love we share."

Gable speaks about the research that documents couples that fight poorly, criticize, and are jealous are most likely to separate.

Honest positive responses (no one knows better than your partner when you're faking it) that promote understanding, validation, and caring are necessary. The reassuring feeling of support gives us confidence that when stress occurs, we, as a couple, can handle it efficiently.

The same friend who said he likes to be admired has been married for 20 years. He confesses that an old person married for many years once told him, "there are times when you look at your partner and think, 'I can't remember why we are still married, I'm not sure that I like you anymore.'"

He said, "I remember that when I look at my wife and think those thoughts, and then I also remember what the old woman said, she said, 'stick it out, build on the positive, you'll probably find it's worth it.' And it's true," he said.

When we celebrate each other's accomplishments, we thrive.

> *"The remarkable thing is that we really love our neighbor as ourselves: we do unto others as we do unto ourselves. We hate others when we hate ourselves. We are tolerant toward others when we tolerate ourselves. We forgive others when we forgive ourselves." – Eric Hoffer*

# ABOUT SHAME

I never felt shame. Ever. I was quite clear in my head from the beginning that it was the rapist that should carry shame, and those in society who fail to act against harm.

Many people harmed carry inappropriate shame. One very religious woman told me of her shame and said she even feared speaking to me about it because it was 'immodest.' I responded: 'Immodest? You have been raped. Somebody (or persons) takes us and brutalizes us, they enter our most sacred space, and they violate us. They cause us to feel disgust at them and at us. There are things that linger in our mind; we have 'strange' fears that suddenly come at us. Sometimes we hate the fact that we can't be as 'normal' as we want to be. And then religion or culture or the insensitive come up with things that hurt us more ... please don't let that happen."

Those who come from very conservative religious communities can fear the response. After fundamentalist

Jewish men upbraided an eight-year-old girl for dressing in a 'seductive manner' a rabbi wrote in the New York Times[7]: "The Talmud, the basis for Jewish law… places the responsibility for controlling men's licentious thoughts about women squarely on the men.

'Put more plainly, the Talmud says: It's *your* problem, sir; not hers.

'The ultra-Orthodox men in Israel who are exerting control over women claim that they are honoring women. In effect they are saying: We do not treat women as sex objects as you in Western society do. Our women are about more than their bodies, and that is why their bodies must be fully covered.

'In fact, though, their actions objectify and hyper-sexualize women. Think about it: By saying that all women must hide their bodies, they are saying that every woman is an object who can stir a man's sexual thoughts… She is not seen as a complete person, only as a potential inducement to sin.

'Of course, once you judge a female human being only through a man's sexualized imagination, you can turn even a modest 8-year-old girl into a seductress and a prostitute.

'At heart, we are talking about a blame-the-victim mentality. It shifts the responsibility of managing a man's sexual urges from himself to every woman he may or may not encounter. It is a cousin to the mentality behind the claim, "She was asking for it."

'So the responsibility is now on the women. To protect men from their sexual thoughts, women must remove their femininity from their public presence, ridding themselves of even the smallest evidence of their own sexuality.

'All of this is done in the name of the Torah and Jewish law. But it's actually a complete perversion. The Talmud, the foundation of Jewish law, acknowledges that men can be sexually aroused by women and is indeed concerned with sexual thoughts and activity outside of marriage. But it does not tell women that men's sexual urges are their responsibility. Rather, both the Talmud and the later codes of Jewish law make that demand of men.

'It is forbidden for a man to gaze sexually at a woman, whether beautiful or ugly, married or unmarried, says the Talmud. Later Talmudic rabbis extended this ban even to "her smallest finger" and "her brightly colored clothing — even if they are drying on the wall."

'To make these the woman's responsibility is to demand that Jewish women cover their hands, and that they not dry their clothes in public. No one has ever said this. At least not yet.

'The Talmud tells the religious man, in effect: If you have a problem, you deal with it… The power to make sure men don't see women as objects of sexual gratification lies within men's — and only men's — control.

'Jewish tradition teaches men and women alike that they should be modest in their dress. But modesty is not defined by, or even primarily about, how much of one's body is covered. It is about comportment and behavior. It is about recognizing that one need not be the center of attention. It is about embodying the prophet Micah's call for modesty: learning "to walk humbly with your God."'

Early in 2012, Afghanistan president Hamid Karzai pardoned a 19-year-old woman who was jailed for 12-years after she was raped[8] by a relative. The rapist was not jailed. Her 'crime' was having 'sex out of wedlock' even though it was not consensual. *The Huffington Post* noted that: "Karzai's office said in a statement that the woman and her attacker have agreed to marry. That would reverse an earlier decision by the 19-year-old woman, who had previously refused a judge's offer of freedom if she agreed to marry the rapist. Her plight was highlighted in a documentary that the European Union blocked because it feared the women featured in the film would be in danger if it were shown." The European Union's decision, ironically, forced her to agree to marry the rapist to obtain freedom from jail. Blocking the ability of those harmed to speak always causes greater harm.

Rape metaphorically poisons us – most of those raped will complain about stomach pain - and the only way to get it out is to speak it out; if we don't it stays in there and festers and brews, it builds. It is not enough to only tell a psychologist or a counselor, it is important that you tell your partner, your parents, those closest to you so they can understand the mood and behavior changes and give you the support you need.

The rapist's influence ends when you end it. The rapist only had power over you for a brief time. Don't extend his power. We have a choice: we leave the rapist/s there on that day, or we carry them forever, but it is *we* that carry them. They no longer remember you. They care nothing for you. Do not bring them into your life and your family.

You need to ask why you *need* to feel ashamed. You have relieved criminals of their shame and you wear it. Why? Why are you not standing up as a glorious woman, a woman beloved by her partner, her children, her family, her God, why do you not say I was raped and I am using that as a gift, a gift to extend healing, to extend compassion, to be a more thoughtful wife and mother? Because it is a gift, if you allow it to be.

To a very religious woman who felt she had shamed her faith, I asked, 'Tell me, what sort of God, and what religion or religious who claim to worship Him would reject anyone harmed? Would you reject one of your children if they were harmed? Of course you would not, so how could you be greater than God?

'God has already given you the opportunity to defeat them.'

She was wounded in the vaginal area during the rape and so I wrote: 'You have two children; the doctors say it is a 'miracle' that you gave birth to them. They are your miracles of life and regeneration. Your babies need their mother with them, not lost in her head, fearful and ashamed about something she had no control over.'

Earlier in her life, a man who asked her to marry him broke off the engagement when he discovered she had been raped as a teenager. His rejection reinforced a sense of shame in her, but I wrote of his rejection: 'For this I hope you give thanks to God every day. Because if you had not told him you were raped, you may have married him - this would have been a selfish, cruel husband. So the rape created a blessing for you.

'Instead you met the gentle man who is your husband, who loves every scar, kisses away every tear, how blessed you are. Do not dishonor that love by allowing the rapist into your home.'

I continued, 'I think God gives us tests to help us become more than we dream we could be. We just think we are average people muddling along and then something awful comes and hits us and we fall back, distraught, wounded. We have options, we can curl up and hope to die; we can crawl into a corner feeling ashamed or resentful and hope no-one sees us (and yet we also want their pity - and pity is the greatest disabler of all), or we can mourn and then say: No, I am not going to let this ruin my life, I am going to seek the lesson, learn from it and use this setback to make my life better, richer...

'And that's hard because we have no idea what the lesson is, and sometimes as we climb up we feel the cliff crumbling under our fingers, but climb we must.

'What are some of the things I have learnt? Life is short; it can go in an instant. The person who raped me could have killed me. The same could have happened to you.

'We need to have positive revenge and we do that by not being bitter or hating, we ignore those that harm. They are meaningless. We focus on *our life*. I tell those I love that I love them often, I express gratitude a lot - for the people in my life and life itself, the plants and trees, the weather ...

'The more good you seek in life, the more good comes to you. The more you show kindness to others, the kinder the universe is to us (that does not mean our lessons are over, heavens no, at the end of last year I was really sick and as I lay in my hospital bed I looked up and said, "God you know I'm getting really tired of the lessons...")'

But still the lessons come. I have a destiny, I have no idea of what, but it is to be more than I am.

You have a destiny too.

We have to find our own meaning.

If you try to understand the motives of those that harm, then you are offering yourself up to a life of inner torture. You will devote yourself to studying those who harmed you, instead of those who blessed you. We have choice.

Don't bring the rapists into your home, into your relationship and into your bed - they are not allowed there.

They are not allowed back into your life.

Not now, not ever.

Get rid of them.

Now.

Forever.

## COMMUNICATION HEALS

Talk to your partner. You don't need to tell him or her everything, but if yours is an intimate relationship they need to know what you are experiencing.

There may be things they do that will make you feel unhappy. Or you may be anxious. If it is soon after your experience of violent harm, go slow, focus on the things that make a relationship last; have great conversations, go for walks, do thoughtful things for each other, focus on strengthening all communication bonds. Is anything nicer than sitting on the sofa holding hands or arms draped around each other, just talking?

Because of the reactions you may have after being raped you may have no desire to resume sex, or you may fear touch, certain smells or sexual acts. Even kissing for those forced to kiss a rapist can be a problem.

Explain to your partner how you feel, if you are nervous about revealing everything you feel to him or her, then do it in a safe environment, in front of a counselor is ideal, especially someone trained in sexual assault counseling or a sexologist. Not all psychologists are adept at sexual assault counseling, so keep trying counselors until you find someone that you feel 'gets you' and the issues you wish to discuss.

The Seattle Institute for Sex Therapy, Education, and Research[9] gives some wise advice (in bold), which I have abridged or added to below:

**_You don't want sexual contact, but do want other forms of physical contact._**

Tell your partner and suggest other ways to be physical, this could include cuddling on the couch, holding hands, a kiss on waking and on sleeping, sitting close, spending time together.

One couple were newly married when one night when the husband came home late from his demanding job, carjackers forced him into the house at gunpoint. His wife was sleeping. They woke her, wrapped him in the duvet and bound him with rope, then gangraped her next to him while he lay helpless.

Afterward John said, "At least I know what a woman now goes through," but he was devastated that he had been unable to stop them coming into their home or from harm coming to her. It took 18 months of therapy with a counselor and then a sexologist and lots of gentle touch (in the beginning sexual touch needs to be avoided), conversation and slowly, slowly moving back toward sex. They now have three boys and are among the happiest couples I know.

Once you feel comfortable with more erotic touch, move into it gently, take a bath or shower together and take turns washing each other. Or cuddle under the covers and gently stroke each other. Go on a massage course together and learn healing touch. Don't forget your favorite music or candles, and pay attention to how it feels to touch and be touched without the pressure to be sexual.

***You are open to sexual contact but are cautious because you don't know what your reactions will be. Certain behaviors, touches, looks, and smells may trigger fear, anxiety, and/or flashbacks (memories of the assault).***

Stop the sexual activity at any time. It's okay to know your limits and act on them. Some couples set up a signal system, for example, a squeeze on the right shoulder means, "Stop now, I'm scared." Or simply say, 'this makes me anxious.'

Before beginning any sexual activity, you may want to say to your partner: "Lots of times I'm not sure how I'm going to react during sex, so I may want to stop even after we've started. I'll try to tell you what I want instead, like different kinds of touching or a different position."

Don't put any pressure on yourself to perform sexually. If there is any physical discomfort as a result of sexual contact, do not hesitate to get a medical examination. Later I discuss a very common cause of vaginal pain – but get an examination anyway, leave nothing to chance in helping your body and mind heal.

*You are open to sexual contact and don't have anxiety, but you become aware of previous sexual issues that you have ignored or avoided (e.g., lack of orgasm, painful intercourse, lack of desire, previous sexual abuse, etc.)*

Tell your partner as much as you know about your feelings and what you want to change, if anything.

Seek help from a therapist who specializes in working with sexual problems. The therapist can help you talk to each other in a constructive manner. If you feel that your partner cannot do this without resentment or pressure, the Seattle Institute recommends that you first deal with issues around trust and respect in your relationship.

Jann, a rape survivor noted: 'It is possible to be intimate with a caring and emotionally stable partner, but not an emotionally insecure or selfish person. If a woman has been raped and then decides that sex is not what she wants to do, or at least not on certain terms, that is okay too. Self-touch and non-sexual intimacy are also powerful avenues for healing and can be safer, if there is physical or emotional damage that is likely to impede a relationship.

'One has to move forward to something else more sophisticated emotionally. Acknowledging the full impact of the rape is just the starting point, but if you can't do that then you can't move on either. A partner may be left feeling helpless at first. But rape is something that happened to us. It doesn't make us lesser people, but it does affect us and always will. It's like breaking your neck: some people will learn to walk again and others won't, and there is room for acceptance of both destinies.'

Jann's words are wise because it is important to understand that the partner's attitude and approach is very important but some trauma survivors can create excuses to remain in victim mode.

The two parties in a relationship need to partner together to develop rewarding intimacy, but most of the work will come from the rape survivor.

If a partner cannot respect your wishes, then it may point to other issues that pre-existed within the relationship. It is too easy to blame everything on the rape, and it can prevent us from breaking through to real solutions. We need to relearn the healing power of intimate touch, and also to never equate rape with sex because that then harms our partner. And us.

# PREGNANCY AS A RESULT OF RAPE

It is estimated that less than five percent of those raped fall pregnant as a result; you are more likely to get a sexually transmitted disease and this is why hospitals and clinics give you antibiotics or penicillin to prevent STD's and the morning after pill to prevent pregnancy.

Children born as a result of rape are at high risk of being rejected by the mother, or abused. In Rwanda, where it was estimated that there was perhaps not a woman nor girl child who avoided getting raped during the April 1994 genocide that saw more than 800,000 die, such children are called, "enfants mauvais souvenirs" (the children of bad memories) and they are looked down upon by society.

For most women being pregnant as a result of rape is a nightmare, she begins hating her body and the child in it.

Yet there are women who love such children, I once spoke to a Washington D.C. personal assistant for a very wealthy man. She was raped when young by another prominent man for whom she worked. She had a daughter, her only child, who she adored and who knew about the circumstances of her birth.

Another woman I consulted with gave up her child for adoption but forty years later began looking for him, and found him. It was traumatic for him to learn that he had been born as the result of rape, but with therapy and a loving new family, both sets of families managed to work toward a bigger family bound by love.

I believe a child has the right to be born of a loving relationship and into a family, or to a mother who happily awaits his or her birth and who will love and treasure that child. This is not about men's rights or women's rights, it is about the rights of the child and most countries in their constitutions agree with the United Nations Declaration on the Rights of Children, that the rights of a child surpass all others.

# HELP THOSE WHO LOVE YOU

*There is strength, wisdom and power in calmness*

The experience of violent trauma harms more than just the person victimized; it wounds everyone who loves the person harmed.

In the years since I was raped and stabbed I know that some of the impact of rape lives on. I have some of the residue of Post-Traumatic Stress – occasional irrational anxieties – I hate driving over high bridges, as an example, but I am consoled that many who have never been harmed experience the same anxiety. While I was living in the high-crime state of South Africa anxiety had a direct impact on my health – but I was not alone, in a country with a murder rate of 49 per day and a rape every 26 seconds the adrenalin created by fear sometimes kept us alive.

I have never linked sex and rape, *ever,* nor should you;

they have nothing to do with each other. But there was a time when intimate touch caused me fear. I dealt with it by going first for reiki – no touch, then advancing to someone who massaged my hands only. She progressed to massage my head, then over time, my head, feet and hands. And over weeks, I trusted her enough to allow her to massage my back too, and over months, to a full body massage and by the time I resumed sex, it was joyous and natural.

Our challenge after trauma is that we do not become addicted to the sympathy we are shown. Our challenge is not to become victims who victimize our families. Our goal is not merely to become survivors, our objective should be to live happier, better lives despite what happened.

Our challenge is not to complete the attacker's aim in attempting to destroy us by finishing the job long after he has gone and forgotten us.

Our challenge is to defeat those who seek to destroy us by living better, stronger, happier lives filled with new meaning and purpose.

It's hard, but it's harder not to.

Many men and women approach me and say they cannot have sex with their partner, they are fearful of men of a certain race or religion (like the person/s who harmed them), they give me a long list of cannot's and every cannot tells me that as they have retreated from those who love them and they have moved closer to the abuser. This is hard to read, but please read it again and reflect upon it.

They carry the attackers with them; they refuse to let them go, even as they push away those who love them.

Every incident of interpersonal violence is unique because people are unique. But the grieving that follows is universal. We cope in different ways; some heal faster, some slower.

If there are unresolved issues before an assault - an unhappy relationship, difficulties at work, a drinking or drug problem, and self-esteem or sexuality issues - they all come to the fore after.

The challenge for survivor and counselor is to separate which issues are a consequence of trauma, and which the experience of harm has exacerbated. It becomes easy to blame everything on trauma as a way of avoiding issues that we were loath to confront before experiencing harm. I need to stress this because often I hear of counselors who become transfixed by the trauma and blame every problem that follows on the traumatic incident, and that is unhelpful. It keeps you swirling in the whirlpool of the trauma and not advancing back into life.

Effective counselors look at the issues a person had *before* their experience of harm and examine how the trauma may have heightened those issues. Violent trauma opens the door we have sealed on every issue we have tried to suppress and it now demands that we deal with that issue. If we don't we can remain trapped in a circle of unhappiness – a relationship that fails, poor concentration at work or school, ongoing anger or depression…

Go back to that which troubled you before, and start healing that. Once you have addressed the issue that has long troubled you – an unhappy marriage, issues around your sexuality, a bullying father, an unsupportive mother, a job you hate - it creates a chain reaction of healing that brings rest to the challenges of today.

Use today's pain as an opportunity to transform your life.

Predators want you to be tearful, to sit with your head down, your arms folded tightly across your chest. Those who harm know they are powerful when they see you lose yourself in alcohol or drugs and sleep with anyone who comes your way because you so have allowed your mind to devalue your body. Terrorism is not just a political act, sometimes the worst terrorism is experienced at home at the hands of someone we should be able to trust. It can only succeed if we remain fearful – and I've experienced the terror of domestic violence, I know how hard it is to get out from under the grip of the incredible fear that starts dominating your life and mind.

Your revenge against the abuser or the hater is by living a happier and better life than you ever dreamed possible *because* of the harm you experienced. Those who harm want you to hate blindly and stupidly as they do – be radical, never hate, be kind, be a healer, be empathetic, you have experienced the harm hate brings, you are uniquely able to show the world the transformative power of self-love.

Fear of relationships after sexual violence or violent trauma either goes to issues of sexuality or trust. Many are so emotionally battered by the violence they have experienced that afterward they only want relationships with super-humans, people who will never reject us, or complain, or be unreliable - in other words, people who are everything we are not.

It's impossible. We have to take risks because a life without loving and being loved is not a life at all. After surviving harm or violence we have to constantly monitor *not* how insensitively others are handling us, as many of us are wont to do, but how sensitively we are handling them.

One survivor said, 'It's so hard, why do we have to do all the work?' And I answered, because it's our life, it means more to us than anyone else, and it's worth it.

*"When you hold resentment toward another, you are bound to that person by an emotional link that is stronger than steel. Forgiveness is the only way to dissolve that link and get free," Inspirational author, Catherine Ponder*

# Post-Traumatic Stress Syndrome

It is critical that you understand Post Traumatic Stress Syndrome. Learn as much as you can about the syndrome and do not go to a psychotherapist unless he or she has proven expertise in Post-Traumatic Stress Syndrome, many will say they do, but don't, it is a complex syndrome.

Know too, that psychotherapists are just people too, if you are unhappy with the first one, try another, and another, until you find someone that you feel is helping you move forward with your life. If you remain trapped in misery for too long, however, the problem may not be with the psychotherapist, it may be that there is a reason you do not want to heal – self-pity can become an addiction too.

A few notes about PTSS. Trauma is like bile. There is only one way to get it out - through the mouth, through speaking about it, not necessarily about the event itself, but the emotions and experiences afterward. Therein too lie difficulties, as Jewish survivors of Nazi concentration camp survivors realized.

Auschwitz survivor and author Primo Levi noted:

*Those who experience imprisonment (or) who have gone through harsh experiences are divided into two distinct categories, those who remain silent and those who speak . . . Those remain silent who feel deeply that sense of malaise which I . . . call 'shame', those who do not feel at peace with themselves, or whose wounds still burn.*

*The others speak ... because at varied levels of consciousness, they perceive in [the trauma] the center of their life, the event that for good or evil has marked their entire existence.*

We speak because we want inhumanity to end, and our lives to begin.

If we have been so wounded, we say, then all are at risk.

The question *why,* which Levi says was directed at those who survived Nazi death camps from those who had never been in them, is a question that is asked endlessly of those of us who have experienced violent trauma. *Why* in itself is a pointless word that can you trap you in the event and disallow healing. Books, movies, TV series too often give us the delusion that there is a reason – fiction carries reasons, reality rarely does. It can be as pointless as the reveler who shoots a pistol into the night sky and the bullet travels through the sleeping community, shatters a window and lodges itself in the brain of a sleeping baby.

I've interviewed over decades political and criminal perpetrators and know that causes are often random. There may have been orders from a senior – a gang leader, military commander. Drugs or alcohol may have been used. They had a weapon – a gun or a knife. You were in the vicinity. The randomness of the crime can increase self-criticism – if only I hadn't walked down that street, spoken to that person, got into that car… The fault is not yours. But please, stop asking why, if you sat across from the perpetrator and asked 'why' most often you will have a response that is a lie, or is cloaked in words to protect you or him. Focus rather on today and tomorrow, rebuilding your life, moving forward.

It is pointless asking the criminal *why,* the question *why* is the challenge society faces. The answer to *why* lies in how much we value the integrity of every living being. Why is not important – *how* you live your life is.

Part of what I believe brings on Post Traumatic Stress is that we walked into death's realm and were given the opportunity to walk out. While we are still in that realm and believe our life is at risk, we can function; but once security is assured and life becomes more certain, our psyche goes into a state of collapse. We allow the fear we kept at bay to enter. We grieve because we touched our mortality and felt how fragile it is.

And so some who survive war, or concentration camps later commit suicide because they consider the lives they are living to be less worthy than the selfless and heroic lives of some of those they saw die.

Protecting our bodies is usually easier than safeguarding our psyches. During war, torture or an assault we survive by maintaining control over our mind - there is nothing we can do about the pain or bodily degradation; our mind is our tool of survival. But afterward our terror becomes such that although our body may heal, our minds threaten to implode.

The brain that helped us survive during the violent act endangers us over weeks, months and years as it returns to the terror, often at when we least expect it.

Many soldiers survive war through the power of their minds, but afterwards cannot cope with the banality of daily life back home. The war has not ended in their minds; a movie reel keeps replaying the horror in their heads.

They can't talk to those around them because their well-meaning and loving friends, lovers or companions will say, "hush, don't talk about it, it upsets you." But talking about it is what we need to do, and in graphic detail as we try to figure out exactly what happened and why we feel so wounded. Those who love us need to listen silently, horrified and hurt though they may be, but that is what we need, because without it we scream in our heads and may become self-destructive.

It is in moving step-by-step, and clutching on to whatever little bits of unlikely help we may find, that we reach the top of the mountain. And once we are at the top, we discover that our mountain is but one of many mountains. It is part of a range. There is no single peak, there is no ultimate high . . . there are many peaks in any great life.

Life is remarkable precisely because we are imperfect; it is in trying to get past imperfections - or in enjoying them - that we truly taste life.

While love bursts unbidden and often unseen into our hearts, heartbreak develops slowly. It is the unpicking of a knitted garment with a pin . . . the shoveling of ashes into a corner, a little pile that grows and grows until the ash swirls around our head and burns our eyes.

*Pain tells us our body is trying to heal, it wants to live.*

If you are on psychiatric drugs as a result of the trauma, consider going to a doctor who will help you get off them. You surrendered control to a violent assailant, don't persist in surrendering control to the pharmaceutical industry. It is really important that you feel in control of all aspects of your life. Do not stop your medications all at once, it can be very dangerous, you need to wean off them under medical care. This is really important, because as you will learn those who experience Post Traumatic Stress have an increased risk of addiction to narcotics or alcohol – and most of all, *you need to own this victory against a violent perpetrator.*


Own your life. The difficulty you may have in sleeping or depression, are normal reactions to a terrifying situation. A sleeping pill is fine but use it no more than three times a week, and for no longer than a month after the incident. More often than that and for a longer period the drug (especially benzodiazepines) starts creating changes in your brain that encourage dependency. If you are reading this and have been on psychiatric drugs for a long time to help anxiety, sleep or depression then get a good doctor to help you get off them.


This obviously does not apply to those with a recognized psychiatric disorder that was diagnosed *before the rape,* for example, bipolar disorder. If you were diagnosed with the disorder after the rape it is highly likely that your doctor did not understand PTSS, and he or she may have misdiagnosed you. Go for a second, third or even fourth opinion – claim back ownership of your body and your mind.

What sort of exercise are you getting? Enroll at a gym or do something like tai chi, yoga or Pilates at least three times a week, or just go for walks or do stretches on your living room floor. You need to start introducing positive endorphins into your body and do things that make you feel good about your body. Research published in 2016 showed that exercise increases blood flow to the brain, which in turn enhances mental alertness and a sense of contentment.

Work out a couple of days a week, starting today, even if it is just a walk – every day. If you struggle to do this, exercise with a friend or get an app on your smartphone, or a Fitbit or similar device to help encourage you.

The symptoms that follow apply equally to those who have experienced any violent trauma including war, domestic violence or rape.

## POST-TRAUMATIC STRESS SYNDROME
### ACUTE

Immediately after the traumatic event and for several weeks, a trauma survivor will experience some or all of the following symptoms:

Intense emotions, including thoughts of suicide.

Physical reactions such as a missed or very heavy period and a high likelihood of miscarriage if pregnant.

Bodily pain, nausea, vomiting, headaches, stuttering, a bad feeling in his or her stomach.

Changes in sleeping habits (you will often see the incident again when you close your eyes, and so you may have difficulty in getting to sleep and staying asleep, or have nightmares).

Disturbed eating patterns, inability to concentrate.

A good worker will have diminished productivity.

A happy person will become stressed and irritable, she will have severe mood swings and sometimes cry for no apparent reason.

## THE REORGANIZATION PHASE

From six weeks to six months or for years.

*   You may change work, phone numbers, move house, and avoid places or people that make you feel unsafe. You may develop intolerance for certain colors, reject friends or family that you feel are unsupportive. You may resist going to see films that display violence, even television news may be upsetting.

*   Nightmares or flashbacks. These are very real and terrifying to the survivor and for anyone who sees you experiencing them. You may be frightened, may scream, cry, bang the walls or floors, repeat certain words; want to flee,

become catatonic, and avoid things that remind you of the trauma including places, people, certain smells.

- Fear and anxiety. You may fear going out at night, being alone, in public places or crowds. Emotional involvement becomes an issue. You start lacking confidence in your abilities at work.

- It is likely that you will become paranoid about security, checking and rechecking that doors and windows are locked.

- Changes in sexual activity. You may resume sexual contact with her partner soon after the trauma, but may begin resisting this by the sixth week. This can be healed, but requires patience and understanding from the partner. Touch is healing and good, but needs to be relearned.

- Inability to cope with family, children, work, money, alcohol or drugs.

- Loss of self-confidence.

Those who are treated with love and support, encouraged to talk about the traumatic event in whatever way they feel comfortable - without being told how to think or behave - will heal over time.

Ultimately, how well a person recovers depends on how well they *want* to recover.

And please, if you are helping a trauma survivor, or a lover, friend or family member then never ever use clichés like 'time will heal' or 'snap out of it' – time does heal but if it is soon after a violent incident they are so overwhelmed they need you to listen more than you speak.

If you haven't experienced the same, or even if you have, don't tell them how to think or feel. Know that each person harmed is unique – you and I can relate to some, but not all of their feelings. So never say, "I understand…" you want to, but you don't.

Not all therapy is helpful, I had one rape survivor, Pumla, who was gangraped, and she suffered from nightmares, eating problems, mood swings, tearfulness, feelings of hatred towards men and problems common to Post Traumatic Stress Syndrome. Seeking help she went to a trauma clinic where the counselor made her repeat the details of the rape each time she visited.

It is believed in some quarters that in persons who have experienced PTSS, the retelling of the story assists them to cope - but it is counterproductive to make them do this each time they go for counseling. Once is enough.

Patients do not need to live permanently within the crisis, they go for counseling to find ways to move away from the crisis and if this does not happen they do what Pumla did - they give up counseling.


## NEVER

In late November 2011, Anne, a drop-dead gorgeous redhead contacted me, she had been married for two decades to the man who was her first lover. Two years into the marriage he left for work early on the farm they owned. He left her sleeping next to their infant daughter, she awoke to the cold muzzle of a firearm prodding her.

There were three home invaders in her room, she pulled her husband's firearm from beneath his pillow and tried to shoot, nothing happened. The invaders grabbed the gun turned it on her and pulled the trigger, nothing happened; they tried again, still nothing. The baby played peacefully.

And that began a process of them dragging her through the house, beating her, loading up household goods and raping her.

The men involved were never arrested – it always has a worse impact on the person raped if the perpetrator/s get away with it.

A few years later she had another child but intimacy between she and her husband never recovered from the rape. She opened her own successful business but would wear long dresses, her small circle of friends mostly belonged to the same bible study group.

Her marriage was falling apart, her husband had an affair, her children were rebellious and she was seeing a psychologist and a so-called expert on Post Traumatic Stress. She was on anti-anxiety medication and sleeping pills. The PTS 'expert' had told her to figure out what the triggers were that set off PTS and to work at eliminating them – such advice is frankly garbage. We have to learn how to function in the world, not to avoid it.

I told Anne: 'Stop looking for triggers, you're wasting your time because at different times there may be different triggers. By searching for triggers you're going to obsess about the rape and that is a really terrible idea. The rape happened at one time in your life, it was awful, you need to manage it now so it no longer harms you, and keep in perspective, that it is a small part of a magnificent life.

'Research PTSS; know what it is, know what it does... When you can feel something coming on try saying to yourself, "I can deal with this, I can deal with this..." Stay away from psychiatric drugs, those with PTSS are at greater risk of dependency, and you need to own every victory, not a pharmaceutical company.

'PTSS does not necessarily manifest as a breakdown or a flashback, it may suddenly be you finding yourself more anxious about coping with something small that normally you would have sailed through. I went through a time where I found myself very anxious on highways, silly, but it is part of a process that PTSS can introduce in us of being fearful ... so what did I do? I kept getting onto highways. The other day I was with my nephew and he said, "You're a pretty fast driver aren't you Charlene?" And that felt like a victory because in the beginning I could barely make it to the minimum speed.

'Be kind to yourself, and stop sweating the small stuff. Stop looking for triggers, they will find you ... and it's fine, if you experience PTSS you can manage it if you train yourself.'

I added, 'Anne, the person we need to manage is your husband. He loves you, he wants to protect you, and he never wants harm to come to you. Knowing that we were raped deeply wounds our partners. Because he loves you so much, he wants no harm, no deep sadness that he cannot comfort to come to you.  Keep letting him know how important he is to you, how well he helps you get through so much in life, find opportunities to laugh more and to show tenderness. Pay particular attention to ensuring a loving and rewarding sex life.  The men in our lives think rape is about sex, we know it is not and can never be.'

Rape emasculates the men in our lives. If your partner is a woman, she feels bewildered and confused.  Keep lines of communication open. Don't allow yourself to exploit concern by becoming demanding.

Show concern and love to them too, they are just people, not saints. Love and communication is most powerful when it is shared.

Influenced by this book and my words to her, Anne told her teenage children about the rape (and no age is too young, an Israeli woman told her four-year-old and when she was looking sad some days later he came and hugged her then went and got a Band-Aid and said: "I'm making mommy better." Empower your children to be compassionate.0

After Ann told me she had informed her children, I emailed her: 'Your children are going to struggle with this; they won't show it because they want to protect you, but it is challenging news. Thank you for telling them, I deal with people who say the rape was the one thing their mother would never talk about (if she had been raped) and it damaged their relationship with her.  It puts up false barriers.  By doing this you show your children that everything is up for discussion, you allow new intimacy, but too, you make it easier for them to approach you with their fears if they ever experience hurt or harm.

'Let your children know they are safe, and show them coping mechanisms. Let them learn that harm can sometimes see us become wiser, kinder and more powerful than before. That we learn from it."

## TELL YOUR CHILDREN

The importance of telling children cannot be overstressed, they know when things are wrong. You create unnecessary distance and fear when you are not open with them. And if any harm comes to them how can they feel confident to come and tell you, when you lacked the love and skill to tell them?

Dr. Barbara Vacarr, the former president of liberal Goddard College in Vermont, told this story when she was inaugurated at the college in May, 2011 [i]: "My father survived the Holocaust – I didn't know that growing up. I knew that there was something that happened to him, but nobody spoke about it. In the silence of his experience, I developed a fragmented narrative about my own life that served as truth. Yet, deep inside of me there were burning questions and a desire to know more.

"The first time that I got an inkling of the depth of my

father's experience, and consequently my own, was as an adult when my husband and I were having dinner at his house, and my husband turned to him and said, "Jack, why do you have a tattoo on your arm? "

"He told what was for me a harrowing and tragic story of the time he spent in a prison camp in Poland and about his narrow escape...I was completely stunned.

"And something happened to me in that moment. All of my life, his inability to speak his experiences had shaped my personal vision of who I am, of who he was, and of the world we shared. I suddenly understood that in the absence of my father's stories, I had shaped him in the image of stereotypes. I had perceived his silence in my life as the helpless weakness of the victim.

"In that moment he completely changed in my eyes. In the emerging fullness of his story he became heroic. I started to see my life and his life in a very different context and developed a hunger to know about that period in our world's history and about the stories of those who lived it...

"Maya Angelou once said, "There is no greater agony than bearing an untold story inside you." The stories that live in silence very often have the greatest power to transform our world and our understanding of it, when we are given an opportunity to share them and to listen to them."

RACISM

Getting back to Anne and her challenges after rape: the rapists had referred to her as "a white bitch" and that had made Anne and her husband, racist. I wrote: 'You already know what you are writing and saying is not sensible. Are you saying there has never been a black person who has been kind to you or your family? I don't believe it. Change your thinking now. The rapists were criminals. If rape is about race why do so many black women, children and men get raped?

'Rape is a criminal act, if a bank robber goes into a bank and says, "you have too much money, I'm going to take some" would the bank start obsessing about the money they give to charities or the bonuses they give to workers? Of course not. They're rapists Anne. What are you giving their words any meaning?

'After I was raped and started campaigning for anti-retrovirals to prevent the Human Immunodeficiency Virus (HIV) in rape survivors there was a surge in rapists telling those they raped that they were HIV+ - they were trying to sow fear. Rape is not just about the act; it is about terrorizing the person raped. If they can terrorize or humiliate they will.

'What is the one big fear of some whites? A black man raping the white woman - it is a racist fear; because rape by anyone is awful, it is the act that is terrible. By taking on their racism you become like them - do you understand what I am saying? They have succeeded in making you obsess about race - so they have won. Anne, how can we ever allow the rapists to win? How can we ever allow them to control any aspect of our mind afterward?

'The gravest danger facing any person raped is that we become like them - bottom crawlers - we carry unreasonable hates and fears.

'A rapist does not feel good about himself, no one who harms does. They want to reduce us to their level. You become like them if they use racist words toward you and then you start thinking racist thoughts.

'Why would you want to behave or think like a rapist?

'Rapists rape because they can. Instead of worrying about them saying it is because you are white, worry about the fact that so many get away with it and *do something* to support either the cops in your community or groups that help those harmed during crime or violence (not just those raped, go and help at a hospital or an animal shelter, sometimes by protecting we increase our feelings of being protected).

'People of all races, religions etc. rape, if we then hate or fear the **group** they come from eg. a white Jew, then we have lost touch with reality. How could I blame all whites or all Jews for what one or four or three people did? You wrote: "I need to know that not all black men go after white women to punish them." Are you really saying *all black men* go after white women to punish them? Of course not. Be angry with the three that raped you, but never ever with all black people, because if you do, then you are just like the rapists, irrational and hating without logic. And frankly if you were black or Chinese or Indian, they would have given another reason.

'Stop listening to what they say, look at what they do, and the fact that they get away with it.

'If you or your husband or children become racist as a result of this attack then you have made the rapists powerful. Why would you want to do that?

'If we are better than rapists, then we don't think or behave in the way that they do.' And then I gave her a suggestion – it was close to Christmas and I suggested that she do something kind for a black stranger every week.

'Every week, find one person who is black and who seems to need kindness and give kindness. It may be a supermarket cashier who looks glum and who you say some cheerful words to lighten her day and make her feel acknowledged. It may be a staff member who you chat to and discover a challenge they are dealing with; consider a way to help them. There are five weeks to Christmas and you are going to make five black people feel better about themselves and at least two need to be men. By Christmas you will have regained your own power and spirit, and you will have defeated the rapists. I need you to trust me on this, try it, and it will work.

I promise.'

Anne followed this advice, she would write or call me telling me about her latest act of kindness. almost giddy with the pleasure it gave her, the warmth she was feeling from others in return.

She took back her power, there is no greater power than that kindness bestows.

It had an impact on every area of her life, her husband who had walked out begged to return, 'how can you change this much in two weeks,' he would ask, and then he stopped asking as he too, inspired by her example, began changing.

# EATING DISORDERS AFTER RAPE

When a rapist or rapists force those raped to kiss them or perform oral sex we cannot disassociate our minds from what is happening. The act takes place before our eyes, and we are forced to confront what is happening. By contrast with rape in the genital area we are able to disengage, many women and men talk of having a sense of disassociation and of 'lifting' out of their bodies.

Orgasm can, on rare occasions, happen during rape, it has nothing to do with sexual arousal. When the body is in a fear-filled mode adrenalin races around the body; it is what helps you to think clearly. Because there is so much adrenalin your body may be ultra-sensitive to certain stimuli. And in the same way that if you walk into a room with dust you will sneeze, the same happens when certain things are done to your body.

In the same way that you could not control the sneeze, you cannot control the orgasm, it is simply an automatic response from your body.

Similarly, some may urinate or defecate during or after rape, it is an uncontrolled response to fear.

Nothing disgusts a woman more during rape than kissing and oral sex. A high percentage of those who are forced to perform oral sex develop eating disorders - they cannot bear to have anything near their mouth. These eating disorders tend to develop as Post Traumatic Stress intensifies, usually around three to six months after the rape.

The impact of post-rape trauma is often delayed. When people are starting to say 'So-and-so is coping so well' may be the time when she or he is battling to cope the most.

Angela was a teacher who was driving home from the movies with a colleague when their car was forced off the road. The attackers beat her colleague before she was kidnapped and then gang raped. She was also forced to perform oral sex. Around four months after she was raped Angela stopped eating. Because she had been forced to perform oral sex she no longer wanted anything to pass through her mouth.

And so I did something with Angela that I have since successfully done with other rape survivors who have eating disorders ranging from bulimia to anorexia – a number of psychotherapists and medical institutes have also adopted this technique and record remarkable success.

I've never yet heard of it failing.

I asked Angela to eat one of three things each day, three pieces of fruit, a peanut butter sandwich or a bowl of homemade soup. She needed to eat only one of those items.

We then began a process of reclaiming her mouth. I ask survivors to buy a new toothbrush and completely different toothpaste from that which they normally use. If they can afford floss or mouthwash that is great too, but warm salt water is also an effective mouthwash.

They must book an appointment with a dentist, or a state or university dental clinic if they have no money, and have every problem in their mouth sorted out.

Then they must buy a lipstick or lip-gloss - it doesn't matter if they don't usually wear lipstick – and they must buy one in a shade they don't normally wear.

These small steps lead to a great reward. This *reclaiming of the mouth* works, the eating disorder goes into abeyance and is ultimately overcome. I told psychologists about this at the Centers for Disease Control in Atlanta and they agreed that there are important psychological reasons why techniques like this work. And as an important note, do it even if you were raped and forced to perform oral sex twenty or thirty years or more ago, if you do it today to reclaim your mouth and your mind, it will work.

Massage also helps, but commence it slowly, go first for a head or foot rub, get used to that, then after a while go for a shoulder and neck rub, later on a back rub and finally a full body massage.

I get some saying they can't because they feel so tense, but often that tension is self-inflected. If one becomes hyper-anxious about anything you destroy any positive impact it may have. Positive self-talk is an important tool of changing negative conduct.

Before you go for your massage tell yourself how wonderful it is going to be, how you deserve it, and relax under that healing touch.

Every day after your bath or shower, stand naked in front of a mirror and look at your body and look at all of its best features, admire it and love it, give thanks for it, and for the life that is in it.

## Domestic violence

All over the world, women find themselves at special risk of HIV infection because of their lack of power to determine where, when and how sex takes place. What is less recognized, however, is that the cultural beliefs and expectations that make this the case also heighten men's own vulnerability.

HIV infections and AIDS deaths in men outnumber those in women on every continent except sub-Saharan Africa, often women cannot negotiate safe sex because of an abusive partner who is also not monogamous.

Married women by far outrank every other category of those most at risk to HIV, or those most infected. UNAIDS tells us that bout 36.7 million people are living with HIV around the world, and as of June 2016, 17 million people living with HIV were receiving medicines – antiretroviral therapy - to treat HIV, called antiretroviral therapy. An estimated 1.1 million people died from AIDS-related illnesses in 2015. While HIV is now a disease easier to control than diabetes, and often with more positive outcomes (no pun intended), the battle against sexually transmitted illnesses like gonorrhea and syphilis is being lost as overuse of antibiotics is seeing an increasing incidence of multi-drug resistant sexually transmitted illnesses.

Part of the effort to curb the AIDS epidemic includes challenging harmful concepts of masculinity and changing many commonly held attitudes and behaviors, including the way men view risk and how boys are socialized to become men. Broadly speaking, men are expected to be physically strong, emotionally robust, daring and virile. Some of these expectations translate into ways of thinking and behaving that endanger the health and well-being of men and their sex partners.

A man at war with himself often takes it out on women.

The National Center for Injury Prevention and Control at the Centers for Disease Control in Atlanta notes that, 'witnessing intimate partner violence (such as one parent beating the other) as a child or adolescent, or experiencing violence from caregivers as a child are the risk factors most consistently identified with the perpetration of intimate partner violence. Men who are physically violent towards their partners are also likely to be sexually violent towards their partners and to use violence towards children.'

The same research shows that very few batterers stick to intervention or education groups, 'with as many as 50% to 75% of men failing to complete the mandated program'.

Do not stay in a bad marriage for the sake of the children; it will scar them for life. Get help now. There are phone lines you can call; there are people you can see. Slowly start putting money away; keep a bag of your clothes and the children's clothes somewhere secret and safe while you prepare to leave. Or call the police and get an order forcing him to remain away from the house.

Know too that the time a woman leaves an abuser is the most dangerous time for her, so ensure others know of your intentions, and have people there to protect you when you take the brave, but necessary step away from someone who harms you and your children.

# Violence Disenfranchises

In her book *The Whole Woman* Germaine Greer wrote: 'We should never have settled for the word feminism instead of women's liberation: What none of us noted was the ideal of liberation was fading out with the word. We were settling for equality. Liberation struggles are not about assimilation but about asserting difference, endowing that difference with dignity and prestige, and insisting on it as a condition of self-definition and self-determination.'

We have forgotten that the keys to any relationship are respect and dignity. We have forgone the societal rituals that denote respect, and so we have lost respect. We are abused in ever increasing numbers because men, with societal strictures removed, are treating us as the undignified creatures the misogynist always believed we were.

Greer notes:

'Women could never find freedom by agreeing to live the lives of unfree men . . . The price of the small advances we have made toward sexual equality has been the denial of femaleness as any kind of a distinguishing character.'

A defining feature of many men is the ability to have sex without emotion – it is contrary to the psychological makeup of women, but heck, 'we're free' some say, 'if they can do it, so can we' and they do, you see them staggering on pavements at night, puking into gutters, and going home with men whose names they don't know. There's no freedom in that. And within promiscuity is the potential for lots of self-harm and too we are seeing the highest figures for violence against women and children than at any other time in history.

Some in the media industry that get rich on disrespecting women. We have been enslaved by our thoughtless adoption of so-called new freedoms.

Sexist advertising (which implies that women are for trade or barter), contributes to a belief that women are available, they are for sale, and those who don't 'play the game' are setting themselves up for punishment at the hands of their partners or other men.

We are now demeaned daily in advertisements, in books, on television and movie screens - and we trumpet this as freedom. Look only at the drunken, sluttish, mean conduct of some women in television reality shows, or the petulant, rich bitches who do nothing of any value and sneer at each other. They make millions demeaning women – and their biggest audiences? Other women. Greer remarks:

'Our culture now depicts much more elaborate violence in more media more often than it did 30 years ago . . . our culture ... is, by my judgment, less feminist than it was 30 years ago. Brutality, like other forms of pornography, damages everyone exposed to it. Violence disenfranchises all weaklings, including children, old people and women.'

*Violence disenfranchises.* We have been given the vote to silence our voices.

Catherine A MacKinnon in her book, *Feminism Unmodified* notes that 'pornography causes attitudes and behaviors of violence and discrimination that define the treatment and status of half the population... In pornography, women desire dispossession and cruelty. Men, permitted to put words (and other things) in women's mouths, create scenes in which women desperately want to be bound, battered, tortured, humiliated and killed. Or merely taken and used. Greater efforts of brutality have become necessary to eroticize the tabooed - each taboo being a hierarchy in disguise - since the frontier of the tabooed keeps vanishing as one crosses it . . . more and more violence has become necessary to keep the progressively desensitized consumer aroused to the illusion that sex is daring and dangerous . . .'

Some internet sites like Craigslist have sections encouraging free sexual encounters with strangers, some of the most popular dating apps are little more than sexual hookups – at least prostitutes have some dignity, if you want to use their body, you pay.

MacKinnon writes: 'Sexual terrorism has become democratized . . . Show me an atrocity to a woman, I'll show it to you eroticized in pornography.' But pornography has become mainstream, barriers have gone, children take videos of each other performing blow jobs, elected officials tweet photographs of their genitals, the human body has become a commodity – yet with a lower value than a commodity, we give it away free.

Excessive drinking by women has become a global health problem and a risk to our personal safety. In the USA, the National Institutes for Health report,
Sixty percent of U.S. women have at least one drink a year. Among women who drink, 13 percent have more than seven drinks per week.
For women, this level of drinking is above the recommended limits published in the *Dietary Guidelines for Americans*, which are issued jointly by the U.S. Department of Agriculture and the U.S. Department of Health and Human Services.
The *Dietary Guidelines* define moderate drinking as no more than one drink a day for women and no more than two drinks a day for men.

The *Dietary Guidelines* point out that drinking more than one drink per day for women can increase the risk for motor vehicle crashes, other injuries, high blood pressure, stroke, violence, suicide, and certain types of cancer.

Hospital emergency rooms are often clogged at the weekends with women so drunk they cannot stand or walk. They often need to be hospitalized and treated to prevent alcohol poisoning, which can be fatal. Women who are so drunk are easy targets for predators.

# FORGIVENESS

In ancient Aramaic, Jesus' language, 'forgiveness' means to untie or let loose. Nobel Peace Prize winner, Nelson Mandela talks about making friends of our enemy.

It's really hard to do. I don't believe we can forgive the crime, but sometimes forgiving the perpetrator can set us free. Personally I'll never be able to forgive the person who raped me, but as part of my studies on restorative justice I wrote a 'forgiveness letter' to my abusive father who had died two years before. I might have felt differently if he was still alive, I will never know, writing the letter in the quiet of an Oakland apartment as the sun was struggling to rise above the city, was transformative for me.

These were my first words, "My first memories of you are fearful, my mother saying, "wait until your father comes home," and yes, long ago I realized what a wicked perpetrator she was. And then you coming home and taking off your belt, the weals on my legs, standing before my brothers to lessen the blows directed at them. Eldest girl children are always little mothers.

"You'd sometimes tell me how proud you were when I was born, how my eyes sparkled, but neither you nor my mother ever told me you loved me." But by the end of the third page, this is how I concluded,

*When you died I received a text message. "Your father died this afternoon." That was it. I didn't respond. I found out bits and pieces over time, that you'd moved into a retirement home, you developed Alzheimer's, and that none of the children you tortured visited you. You died alone.*

*I kept thinking about my absence of feeling. A few months after your death, Mandela died and I mourned deeply. I still do. And that made me reflect on my absence of feeling for you, and then at Christmas 2013, snow began falling in New England and I thought of how sad your life was, how narrow it had been, how blessed I was to love many and be loved by many. And the hate left me and sorrow for your sad life is what I now have, and so dad, my father, the architect of the person I am today, I want to say thank you and I hope you have at last found peace.*

It was in writing the letter that I realized having a bigoted father, saw me despise discrimination and embrace diversity. Experiencing harm at his hands made me empathetic. Cruel parents made me a good mother – my parents were my barometer, what I saw as their failures, I tried hard not to repeat. My experience of being raped saw me become an outspoken advocate for the rights of women, I was already an advocate for the rights of children. It led me to research masculinity, to ponder how we raised our boys, and I became involved in volunteer work in prisons because I wanted to be part of 'the change I wanted to see' – as Gandhi suggested. If I can help just one person turn away from self-harm and harming others, then my entire life has been worthwhile.  In Judaism it is known as Tikkun Olan, changing the world by working for the benefit of others – or even just one person. In Islam it is a dictum to help those who lack your blessings.

The harm we experience can destroy us, or become the implement we use to improve the world or ourselves (or both). Here are some thoughts on forgiveness:

*"To forgive is to set a prisoner free and discover that the prisoner was you."– Lewis B Smedes*

If you can't forgive then work on forgetting, or rather, never hating.

"I didn't need to forgive that person who publicly called me a bossy person – I needed to forgive myself for not being the sweet demure person I'd like to be but am not. I didn't need to forgive that ex-boyfriend who cheated on me – I needed to forgive myself for poor judgment and not seeing the signs. It was never about them; it was always about me. Once I accepted and forgave myself, there was nothing left to do – I had forgiven them in the same act of forgiving myself."- blogger Joyful Insights

# Reclaiming your sexuality

Soon after I was raped, I encouraged people to hug me. I was not in a relationship and thought I had no problem with touch. But a month later I went for aromatherapy and the minute the female aromatherapist touched my legs I felt panicky. I said nothing to her because I did not want her to feel responsible for my fear.

At one stage my body was trembling so badly that she brought in infrared lamps because she thought I was cold. I realized I was now frightened of intimate touch. I told myself: the rapist is not going to take that away from me too. I deliberately began going for facials and foot rubs and head rubs so I could relearn that touch was good and healing. Explore alternative therapies like Reiki, aromatherapy, facials, foot rubs or reflexology, whatever you need to relearn healing touch.

And there is something so simple you'll laugh when you read it. About six weeks after I was raped my hairdresser called me and offered to treat me to a haircut and color for free. Although I was exhausted and tense, I went to his salon. He made mine the last appointment of the day so that they could tend to me in a quiet and calm salon. He and his assistant treated me with love and care. As a gift, he cut my hair short and highlighted. Often throughout the next year, when I was feeling really low, he would treat me. I looked different, and it gave me a confidence boost.

Ever since then one of the first things I suggest a rape survivor do is to go to the hairdresser, it sounds silly, but little has a better impact. And always get something done that is completely different to your normal style, there needs to be a different you looking back from the mirror, we have great difficulty at looking at the woman who was raped. So change the way you look and you will feel a remarkable lifting of your spirits too.


Now getting back to actually having sex again; the sort of partner you choose is vital if you are not already in a relationship.


There is a school of men who believe they are good men, that they know what we need, leave it up to them, they will care for us, protect us, make us happy. But they are often men who have never had a real conversation with a woman. He has never sat down with a woman and talked to her as a friend, he has never *heard* her needs. He has no realization that if he helps fulfill her needs, she will reward him by helping to fulfill his. Love is a process where we learn tolerance and forgiveness, of the other and ourselves, where we learn how to make each other happy, how to heal hurts and build trust. It is that process of building trust and confidence that allows us to talk and listen during sex and about sex, that helps us to give and share pleasure. It is an evolution of the self, a process of learning and mutual enrichment.

Then there is a group that regard women only as potential sexual conquests – and so they will never give, or receive, really good sex. They think sex is about their needs – not about the celebration of a good relationship.

Apart from the fact that you experienced a violent attack, part of what makes rape so extraordinarily repulsive is its static coldness. Rape is programmed and empty, it is mechanical and devoid of humanity. Rape is not sex. Perhaps that is why so many rapists have profound erectile dysfunction.

There are some, particularly when it comes to date rape who will say, 'there comes a time when a man can't hold back,' and so they display the most profound problem of the sexually incompetent, and therefore the eternally frustrated, male. A lack of control. Because good sex is all about self-control.

Once when discussing this on radio after a man had said: 'there comes a time when a man can't hold back,' I asked,

'Is he suggesting that if he was in a public place and felt a need to urinate he would simply wet his pants?'


*Sex is about self-control.* It is about finding the little keys that turn a partner on, it is about creating desire, it is about holding back one's own desires to please a partner, confident in the belief that he or she will do the same for you, until both achieve mutual satisfaction - and desires.


Sex is a gentle sharing, mutual pleasure, and awareness of the self and the other; it is a gift of trust and the fulfillment of self-worth.


*Sex is about mutual respect.*

Research among orangutans, quoted in Richard Wrangham and Dale Peterson's *Demonic Males: Apes and the Origins of Human Violence,* has shown that 'most rapes are done by a special kind of male that increasingly appears to be a freak of the ape world: an adult male frozen in an adolescent's body'. I suspect that if research was done among human rapists something similar would be found: their levels of maturity and responsibility will be low; their interest in pornography will be above average; their capacity to restrain their temper, even among the seemingly most mild-mannered, will be poor; their need for acceptance will be high. They are men who have grown up physically, but are mentally trapped in adolescence.

The victimization syndrome around rape survivors expects us to crawl into a hole and always be damaged and mournful wouldn't it be nice if we became triumphant? If we stood up and said proudly, I have no shame; I hurt no one and never will, I am triumphant because he or they wounded my body, but they never, never touched my soul, they could never take my spirit.

One young man raped as a teenager said: 'I keep wondering about my future sexual relations: Will the rape permanently affect me?

'Should I avoid sex altogether? Should I just go ahead and pretend nothing happened? It's an uncomfortable topic. I tried dating once and got engaged in sex but it made me feel out of control like the during the rape. It was unpleasant and frightening.'

And that is part of what you need to win back: trust. Rape occurs when someone removes control from us and for many rape survivors regaining control and then never letting go becomes crucial.

Sex and love are about trust, it is about each surrendering to the other and knowing that with this person I am safe, and they are safe with me.

It is honoring the body of your lover as you know he or she will honor yours.

Daniel continued: 'I really don't do relationships well. I become too assertive.' Which again displays the lack of trust he has in his partner, which in effect is an echo of the lack of trust he has in himself.

'You know it has been 10 years since my ordeal and I still have nightmares and panic attacks. It has affected my mental and physical health [he was diagnosed HIV+ after the rape], my performance at work and school, and my relationships with friends, with family, and with lovers. You can heal, you can move on, but once it has happened, it is a part of you for the rest of your life; it never leaves, never changes, and it is never, ever funny - I sometimes try to laugh at the 'off moments'.'

His experience was not dissimilar to another young man raped, Paul, a gifted graduate student was in a relationship for two years before the rape. But his girlfriend's response was like that of many men, she couldn't understand his mood swings, she thought that 'time would heal' and that he just needed to 'get over it.'

Her attitude increased his difficulties with intimacy, he said: 'Sex is so hard now. She wants it but I don't care, I've become worried that I could hurt her and often I experience sexual dysfunction – I can get an erection but cannot sustain it.'

Our psyche is wounded, but it is the spirit that wills us on to survive, to be triumphant. Claim back your sexuality, be a total man or woman again, someone tried to harm you, don't allow that incident to harm loving relationships, love yourself, love your body and allow a good person into your life to show you the love you deserve.

## Cautions before resuming sex

If you went to a doctor, emergency room or clinic after experiencing violent trauma they would have given your medicines to prevent sexually transmitted diseases including HIV from the rapist or rapists.

If you have not been to a doctor, then you must before you resume sexual intercourse. If you have itching in the genital area, sores, an unusual discharge or any changes in the genital area or mouth (if forced to perform oral sex) then see your doctor.

It is advisable to use a condom for the first six months after rape to prevent transmitting a sexual infection to your partner, even if you went onto preventative medication which is known as post-exposure prophylaxis or PEP.

Most sexually transmitted diseases can be avoided if

you went on to medications shortly after the rape and stuck to the course of treatment.

In a small number of cases you can still have an outbreak of an STI, and HIV can occur, if you did not go onto post exposure prophylaxis. The virus can hide and only be found in tests as long as six months afterward, and in a very small percentage of cases, as long as a year afterward.

If you want to know more about STI's ask your doctor, a sexologist or consult the the Centers for Disease Control website.

# PAIN DURING SEX

If your doctor has cleared up any injuries as a result of the rape eg. if objects were forced into you, and if he or she has said you are now fine to resume intimacy you should have no problems.

Sometimes women can experience pain when they resume sex after rape, the good news is that this is most often psychological and is something called vaginismus.

### COMMON SYMPTOMS OF VAGINISMUS

Burning or stinging with tightness during sex

Difficult or impossible penetration, entry pain, uncomfortable insertion of penis

Unconsummated marriage


Ongoing sexual discomfort or pain following childbirth, yeast/urinary infections, STDs, IC, hysterectomy, cancer and surgeries, rape, or menopause


Sexual pain of unknown origin, with no apparent cause


Difficulty inserting tampons or undergoing a pelvic/gynecological exam


Spasms in other body muscle groups (legs, lower back, etc.) and/or halted breathing during attempts at intercourse


Avoidance of sex due to pain and/or failure


Vaginismus is vaginal tightness causing discomfort, burning, pain, penetration problems, or complete inability to have intercourse.


   This vaginal tightness results from the involuntary tightening of the pelvic floor, especially the pubococcygeus (PC) muscle group, although you may not be aware that this is the cause of your pain and difficulties.

Often even just knowing it is psychological is enough for you to resume sex and discover that there is no pain.

No *pills are needed,* your doctor will suggest some pelvic floor and dilation exercises that are easy, non-invasive and simple.

Such pain does not only happen to women raped, it can occur in those who grew up with lots of taboos around sex, it can happen in women who have just given birth to their first child, it is exceedingly common and thankfully, easy to heal.

## Practical Steps to Intimacy

This may have been the page you skipped to first. Read it, but go back and read the whole book, healing is an accumulation of many little things, there is no single quick fix.

If you take these steps, preferably in the order they are listed, you will return to a loving relationship with your partner, or prepare yourself for the sort of quality relationship you deserve.

Ideally let your partner read these notes too. Be open with him or her. Have a least one joint counseling session together with your sexologist, psychologist, counselor or religious adviser.

During counseling you don't have to discuss anything you don't want to. You really don't. But you need to move forward and you're not going to do that by remaining silent or not saying the words that hurt when they come out. You've been through worse pain; this now, is about conquering the harm and living a happier life.

If you find it hard to talk about it, write it. One rape survivor had great difficulty using the words 'sex' or 'rape' and could not tell her husband or her counselor what her challenges were.

I suggested she make up a song about sex, 'sing it when on your own, in the bath, doing housework, whatever, and these are the words I suggest: "Sex is love, sex is trust, sex is my husband loving me, sex is me honoring my man, my family and my future."' It made her laugh – and laughter is one of the doors to healing – and slowly, shyly she would first hum it, then sing it to herself, as soft as a lullaby and later as loud as a revolutionary's protest.

Open yourself to new experiences, different ways of thinking and feeling.

## A NEW YOU

It's a sad reality that people who haven't been loved adequately in childhood are often loved inadequately as adults.

Children tune into the messages they receive from their parents. If parents are distracted, overwhelmed by life, emotionally or financially burdened, they often can't give their children the kind of attention, love and care necessary to thrive.

Although a parent may deeply love a child, saying they love the child just isn't enough. Parents who actively demonstrate love and care on a regular basis tend to raise children who are naturally drawn to healthy love in adulthood.

Through self-love and self-compassion, you can give yourself that which you never received. *The more you learn to value yourself in these ways, the more you will be attracted to people who can love you in a gratifying manner.*

Instead of going around in circles in negative life patterns by dating the same types of people and hoping for different results, stop dating altogether for a period of time. Consider, instead, working to build yourself up from the inside out. Many I talk to tell me: "Okay I get it, but what do I do? How do I start to love myself?"

**Spend Time Alone Each Day.** If you never felt adequately loved, then being alone can create anxiety. You were never taught how to be kind and friendly with yourself, so you avoid yourself. This pattern of avoiding you, however, perpetuates a low self-esteem spiral. Commit to one hour a day when you are by yourself. Spend this time writing in a journal, meditating, or finding ways to be with yourself that are peaceful and comfortable. If you don't take the time, you never give yourself the opportunity to figure out what you need to feel safe and secure standing alone.

**Tools:** Get a meditation app, I like Insight Timer.

Go to free talks or events at bookstores or libraries.

Investigate faith groups and the community around them.

The New York Times has an entire section on meditation including how to do it, guided meditation etc.

**Talk to Yourself Compassionately.** Pause from time to time to pay attention to what your internal narrative is telling you about you and your life. Negative self-talk will lead to unhappiness, doubt and insecurity. We all have a little voice in our heads that comments, judges and draws conclusions about our lives and about ourselves. Start noticing yours. Work to make it less judgmental and kinder, be more appreciative of the positive that you do, so that you can start connecting to yourself in a warm and loving manner.

**Tools:** Keep a Journal

Take walks

Take up photography, it helps you view the world around you in fresh new ways

Start a blog or podcast

**Develop A Hobby or Interest That's All Yours.**

If you have struggled with low self-esteem, it may be hard at first to allow yourself to come up with what you want to do because you think you won't be good enough. Consider volunteering, a fitness goal – taking part in a marathon or a 5K walk. Perhaps you take a part-time job. Anything that helps you connect with feeling competent and effective will make a difference. It's not about being perfect; it's about doing something that makes you feel good about yourself.

**Tools:** Look for courses at adult education centers, museums, local colleges. Free educational courses include Ed-X, Coursera and Khan's Math's Academy.

Correctional institutions are always looking for volunteers to help teach courses ranging from assisting prisoners to complete high school education, to religion, writing, prisoners reading books for their children.

**Make Your Own Decisions.** When you struggle with low self-worth, you come to feel as if you don't know what's best for you. Feeling at a loss, you use others to guide and steer your course. When you can't decide on what to do or not to do, sit with the angst. Even if you make the wrong decision or make a mistake, it's still a success because it was your decision and you were working for your own best interest.

BUILDING THE HAPPINESS JIGSAW

- Put together three to five things that remind you of the traumatic event – it might be an item of clothing you were wearing, the lipstick you wore, it might be a newspaper cutting, a bus ticket, an object the attacker used, and give them away to charity or burn them. As you do say a prayer or an affirmation, perhaps, "I give these away (burn them) to make room for the new in my life."
- Have a very special bath, put salt in the water to soften it, or bubbles or oil, and gently soap your body, show love and caring to yourself. Don't

scrub, just gently soap or sponge.

- Dress with care, nicer than you have for a while. It can still be jeans and a t-shirt if that is what you prefer, but choose your clothes with care. Others need to see the self-love you are showing to yourself, and you need to feel it.
- Book an appointment for a change to your hair – cut it, highlight it, dye it, curl it, straighten it, have braids or dreadlocks, do something different.
- Buy a different toothpaste, toothbrush, to what you usually have. Get a new lipstick or lip-gloss in a color different to what you normally wear. If you never normally wear anything on your mouth, get something clear – gloss or balm and wear it for the next month, that's all it needs. If you wear it for longer that is your choice, but make a month long commitment to yourself.
- Treat yourself to a facial – or give yourself one, make a mask by adding warm water to oats and putting it on your face for 10 minutes, then washing it off. Put lemon juice or tea tree oil on breakouts. Use a good cream on your skin.
- Get a manicure and pedicure or do it yourself. Get used to being kind to yourself.

- Pick or buy flowers or leaves and keep placing them in your home for at least the next month, they bring positive energy into your environment. Perhaps go to a garden center and choose a pot plant that you really like and care for it well – because how well it does is an indication of how well you will care about you.
- Play happy or light music at least once a day, classical is a good option, especially baroque by Mozart or Beethoven, which research shows can improve mood and focus. Perhaps play it when you wake up, or put on something soothing before you go to bed.
- If I struggle to sleep I use a guided sleep meditation from Insight Timer, the free meditation app on my smartphone. Good sleep will start having a definite positive impact on your mood.
- Care for your body, care for your spirit: if you are not going to counseling, find out if there is a good counselor near you. Perhaps you don't want to go to a psychologist, you might prefer a religious or spiritual adviser who won't be judgmental, or is there a group you might enjoy, get among people doing

positive things?

- Exercise daily; even if it is just a half hour walk. If you are disabled, there may be other exercises you can do, but do them, they raise endorphins, which in turn send positive messages to your brain. As fresh blood starts circulating in your body and inches start peeling off, or your muscles get toned, you'll start feeling great.
- Go to a sexologist to improve your sense of sexuality or read books about loving relationships. Authors I recommend include Harville Hendrix and David Richo.
- Go for a massage, if you are very nervous about touch, go first for a foot massage or a head massage, and then slowly – over days or weeks – work up to a neck massage, then a shoulder massage, after that a back massage, and finally a full body massage. Relearn that touch is pleasurable and healing.
- When you bath or shower, take your time, lather your body well, spend time taking calluses off feet, clip your nails, carefully clean those areas where sweat or dirt can gather. Show love and respect to your body. Oil or cream it well afterward.
- Take extra care of your home and work environment, keep it neat, clean

and looking good. The way your home and desk look is a reflection of the inner you – yeah, clean it now!

- Show tenderness to your partner, thank him or her for their support. Put notes thanking them or expressing love in unexpected places where they will find them – a desk drawer, a much-loved book, their IPad cover, a shirt pocket, or write it by hand (remember how to do that?) and seal it in envelope, put a stamp on and mail it to them. Giving is liberating and strengthening.

- Eat healthily – the rapist/s disrespected your body, you need to get into a program of respecting it and showing it extra care every day. My favorite new cookbooks in recent times were Ruth Riechl's *My Kitchen Year*, *Paleo Chef* by Pete Evans, Anna Jones' *Modern Way to Eat, Eat Drink Paleo* by Irina Macri. Each month I'm thrilled when my copy of *Bon Appetit* finds its way into my mailbox, and *Epicurious.com* and *New York Times Cooking* are essential apps on my phone.

- Cook a special meal for your partner, even if you are useless in the kitchen, set a romantic table, they'll know the effort you made and appreciate it.

- Each day for the next month do or

say one kind thing each day to a stranger. Smile at someone in the elevator, help an old lady with her shopping bag, be appreciative to a cashier, shovel snow for a neighbor, clear out your cupboards and donate what you don't need to charity or someone who needs it.

- If you're struggling to sleep start a sleep routine, buy pajamas or a nice nightie, have a bath to relax your body, afterward have half a glass of milk with two cardamom pods boiled in it, go to bed with clean and attractive bed linen, place lavender in the pillows, read a soothing book then switch off your light at more of less the same time each night. Soon your body will – close to that time – start feeling sleepy and you will need no artificial aids to sleep.
- Take risks
- Dare to be unconventional
- Each night reflect on, or give thanks for, six good things that happened that day, it might be something as small as the weather or a person that smiled at you or who you smiled at, or the fact that you have a bed to sleep in. But give thanks.
- Put out seed or suet for birds as the weather gets colder.
- Take a walk

- Invite someone you don't know well, but find interesting for coffee

# MY RELATIONSHIP IS FALLING APART

What may have happened is that even though you are changing in all sort of positive ways, your partner may have already decided – before you started this process of change that she or he wants to walk out the door.  My advice?

*Change, change, change.*

Even if you lose him or her; you need to prepare your life for magical changes. And they will come in abundance if you persist with self-love and positive change. You'll notice first the changes in your children (if you have any) and friends - who will initially be a bit bewildered if you are different but they will respond to you with increased love and respect.

You may find some resistance from friends, especially other trauma survivor friends who may be trapped in victim mode. If we find being a victim works for us - lots of attention from family and friends, we use it.

The problem with being a victim is that over the long-term family and friends (if they have good self-esteem) get frustrated, they start saying to themselves, 'I'm sick of this, I try so hard and s/he just never gets better.'

And that may be where your partner is now, he or she doesn't believe in any change for the better initially, he or she thinks you're going to revert back to being the sighing, miserable victim.

It is going to be hard for you to not revert back to being a victim – it was so pleasurable, for a time, so many took such great care of you (for a time, until they too became depleted by your inability to move forward). If you work through the list in the previous chapter, doing as many of the aspects as you can, perhaps trying a new one each day, then within six weeks you will feel so good about yourself you'll feel like standing on mountains and yodeling.

Some of the advice from your counselor or other books may contradict mine, it's fine, do what works for you. But work on changing your life and not just healing but being incredible; work harder on this than you have ever worked on anything in your life.

It is important to slowly start letting people know you were harmed and how it damaged you. Tell them some of the detail. Tell them how hard you are working now to improve your life and to heal. The best people will come to your aid and be a powerful source of empathetic support.

If you are thinking of moving home or work, wait a while and see if after you have implemented the changes you still want to make the change.

If you decide to move or change jobs, try not to couch it in a way to staff and family of, "I don't feel safe there" – rather say something like this: "I am feeling so positive about the future and the great work from my staff, that I believe we deserve better and more professional offices." Or, "I've seen a beautiful new condo, that is close to the bus route, I have decided I will save more money taking public transport and so I am going to move." In this way you are showing a different, more positive approach. Change the energy around you to being bright and positive.

Walk carefully through your home and office and look for anything that points to negative energy. Anything. Remove it, throw it away. It may be books about crime, or women being unsafe, it may be slogans or pictures. Maintain positive energy in your surroundings, flowers bring that and so do plants, for every negative thing you remove, introduce something positive.

Write a two-page letter to God, a higher power or yourself, giving thanks for everything you are grateful for, every good thing that you have achieved, every good thing from your partner and children and friends.

Then write another one or two pages saying, dear God, please help me bring this into my life... and give a list of achievements in your life with regard to health, happiness and success for yourself, your family and your business. Read the letter once over - it must be handwritten. Then place it in an envelope, kiss it, say a prayer, and put it in a drawer and look at it again only in a year's time.

I promise you, you will marvel at the changes for the better in your life and many will echo the changes you asked for.

There is no time to waste, you've read this far, the time to begin is now. The world is eager for your return.

## Building Happiness

I once counseled an executive banker who felt her life had fallen apart. In her early 50s she'd had an exceptionally successful career, a failed marriage, but had been fired from the last two jobs. "I don't know how to be happy," she said.

Outwardly she had everything going for her, attractive, a great figure, a lovely home but she didn't know how to listen. Her psychic wound was a deep desire for acknowledgement. She would get a great new job and go in like a harvester, reap and whipping what she thought was chaff into the air, carving her way through the company, focused on the people at the top, inwardly saying, "look at me, look at me, look at how hard I work, what a great job I'm doing for the company…"

But along the way she was alienating everyone. She treated low level workers with disrespect, she thought she knew better and could do better than anyone else, and so

behind her back her colleagues conspired to have her fired –
and succeeded – twice.

She'd forgotten an important lesson: we get
acknowledgement, when first we acknowledge others. It may
be empathetically listening to the woes of a colleague. It may
be commenting on the new nail polish of the office
receptionist, "that shade really suits you Bronwyn!" It might
be sending someone a note for a job well done or
congratulating them on a life event that is important to them,
for example, a marriage, the birth of a child, buying a new
home. Pay attention to those around you, encourage them, be
kind and they will go out of their way to do the same a
hundredfold for you.

Norway is consistently ranked in the top three of the happiest
countries in the world – along with Denmark and tiny
Bhutan. The University of British Columbia's co-director of
the Canadian Institute for Advanced Research, John
Helliwell notes, "In Norway, it's quite common for people to
paint each other's houses even though they can all afford to
pay to have their houses painted. They go out of their way to
help each other, and it becomes a social event, and those
events are enormously supportive of well-being. *In the
commercialization of activity - when people are more likely
to buy things than to do them for themselves and each other -
we lose something along the way."*

Loyalty is given to the empathetic – and not the fake empathetic, we've all dealt with those with plastic smiles and clichéd phrases and hated them.


Happiness comes from the unexpected.


'STILL I RISE' BY MAYA ANGELOU


*You may write me down in history*

*With your bitter, twisted lies,*

*You may trod me in the very dirt*

*But still, like dust,*                    *I'll rise...*

*Did you want to see me broken?*

*Bowed head and lowered eyes?*

*Shoulders falling down like teardrops...*

*You may kill me with your hatefulness,*

*But still, like air, I'll rise.*

*Does my sexiness upset you?*

*Does it come as a surprise*

*That I dance like I've got diamonds*

*At the meeting of my thighs?...*

*Leaving behind nights of terror and fear*

*I rise Into a daybreak that's wondrously clear*

*I rise*

*I rise*

*I rise*

*I rise.*

## HELP

* Center for Disease Control's Injury Center
http://www.cdc.gov/violenceprevention

* Information about sexual violence:

http://www.cdc.gov/violenceprevention/sexualviolence/

Intimate partner violence prevention:
http://www.cdc.gov/ViolencePrevention/intimatepartnerviolence.

*If you or someone you know is the victim of:*

Sexual violence, contact the Rape, Abuse, and Incest National Network⬚ (RAINN) hotline at 1-800-656-HOPE.

Intimate partner violence, contact your local battered women's shelter or the National Domestic Violence Hotline at 800-799-SAFE (7233) or visit the National Domestic Violence Hotline⬚ website.

---

[1] Help After Sexual Assault, National Health Service, United Kingdom
http://www.nhs.uk/Livewell/Sexualhealth/Pages/Sexualassault.aspx

[2] Sexual Violence, Stalking, and Intimate Partner Violence Widespread in the US:

New survey finds these types of violence affect the

health of millions of adults, Centers for Disease Control and Prevention, December 14, 2011 http://www.cdc.gov/media/releases/2011/p1214_sexual _violence.html


[3] Bureau of Justice report http://bjs.ojp.usdoj.gov/index.cfm?ty=tp&tid=31

[4] Bureau of Justice report http://bjs.ojp.usdoj.gov/index.cfm?ty=tp&tid=31

[5] RAINN rape statistics http://www.rainn.org/statistics

[6] Men who are raped are the most under-served of all, this site in the United Kingdom is devoted to helping men who have experienced rape or sexual abuse http://www.survivorsuk.org/

[7] Lechery, Immodesty and the Talmud by Dov Linzer, January 19, 2012

[8] Hamid Karzai, Afghanistan President, Pardons Imprisoned Rape Victim, by Deb Reichman, Huffington Post, December 1, 2011 http://www.huffingtonpost.com/2011/12/01/hamid-karzai-afghanistan_n_1123656.html